HAL•LEONARD

Pro Vocal®
BETTER THAN KARAOKE!

SONGBOOK & SOUND-ALIKE CD
WITH UNIQUE *PITCH-CHANGER*™

KATY PERRY

Cover photo: Jake Bailey/August

ISBN 978-1-4768-6877-6

HAL•LEONARD®
CORPORATION
7777 W. BLUEMOUND RD. P.O. BOX 13819 MILWAUKEE, WI 53213

In Australia Contact:
Hal Leonard Australia Pty. Ltd.
4 Lentara Court
Cheltenham, Victoria, 3192 Australia
Email: ausadmin@halleonard.com.au

Visit Hal Leonard Online at
www.halleonard.com

Firework

Words and Music by Katy Perry, Mikkel Eriksen, Tor Erik Hermansen, Esther Dean and Sandy Wilhelm

of ___ Jul - y. ___ 'Cause, ba - by, you're a fi - re - work, __

___ come on, show 'em what you're worth. __ Make 'em go, __

"Ah, ah, ah," as you shoot a - cross the sky - y - y. ___

Ba - by, you're a fi - re - work, __ come on, let your

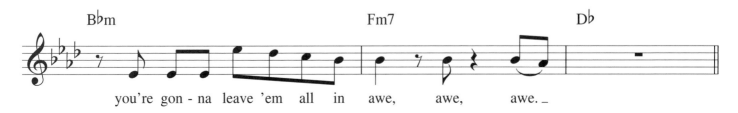

col - ors burst. __ Make 'em go, __ "Ah, ah, ah,"

you're gon - na leave 'em all in awe, awe, awe. __

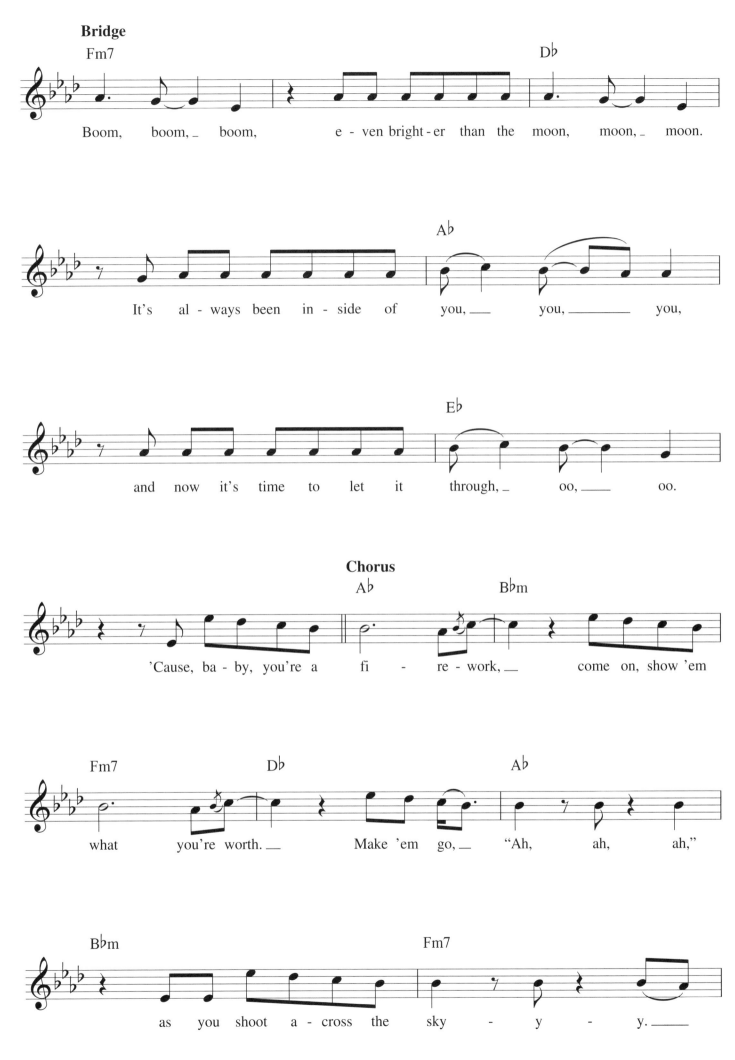

I Kissed a Girl

Words and Music by Katy Perry, Cathy Dennis, Max Martin and Lukasz Gottwald

Chorus

I kissed a girl, ___ and I liked _ it, ___ the taste of her

cher - ry chap - stick. I kissed a girl ___ just to try ___ it. ___

I hope my boy - friend don't mind _ it. It felt so wrong, _

___ it felt so right. ___ Don't mean I'm in ___ love to - night.

I kissed a girl, ___ and I liked _ it, ___

I liked _ it. ___

Verse

No, I don't e - ven know _ your name, ___ it

C   Dm   F5

It felt so wrong, __ it felt so right. ___ Don't mean I'm in __

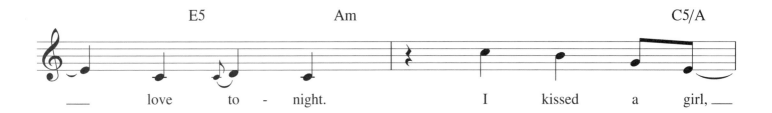

E5   Am   C5/A

__ love to - night.   I kissed a girl, ___

Dm/A   F5/A E5/A Am

__ and I liked __ it, _____   I liked __ it. _____

Bridge

F   Em   Am

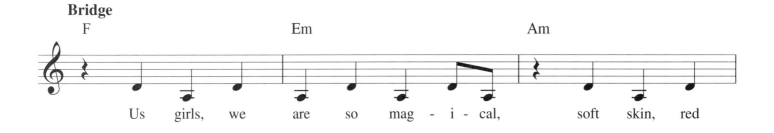

Us girls, we are so mag - i - cal,   soft skin, red

G   F   Em

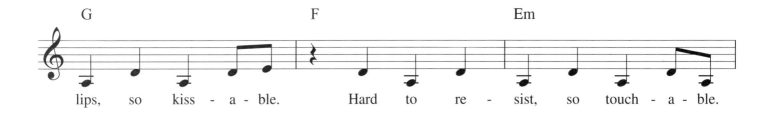

lips, so kiss - a - ble.   Hard to re - sist, so touch - a - ble.

Am   G   Dm

Too good __ to _____ de - ny ___ it. _____ Ain't no big

deal, it's in - no - cent. _____

Chorus

I kissed a girl, ____ and I liked _ it, ____ the taste of her

cher - ry chap - stick. I kissed a girl ____ just to try ___ it. ____

I hope my boy - friend don't mind _ it. It felt so wrong, _

___ it felt so right. ___ Don't mean I'm in ____ love to - night.

I kissed a girl, ____ and I liked ____ it, _____

I liked ____ it. _____

Last Friday Night

(T.G.I.F.)

Words and Music by Katy Perry, Bonnie McKee, Lukasz Gottwald, Max Martin and Benjamin Levin

Chorus

trois. Last Fri - day night. ___ Yeah, I think we broke the

law, al - ways say we're gon - na sto - op, oh, whoa. ___

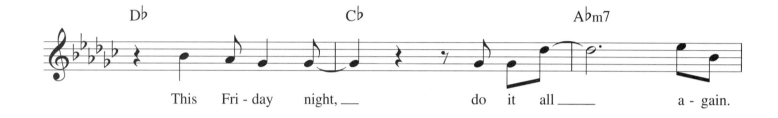

This Fri - day night, ___ do it all ___ a - gain.

This Fri - day night, ___ do it all ___

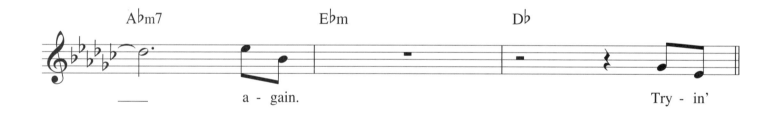

___ a - gain. Try - in'

Verse

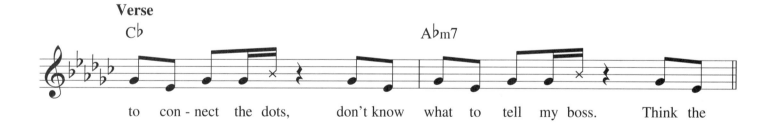

to con - nect the dots, don't know what to tell my boss. Think the

cit - y towed my car, chan - de - lier is on the floor. Ripped my

Chorus

a - gain.

Interlude

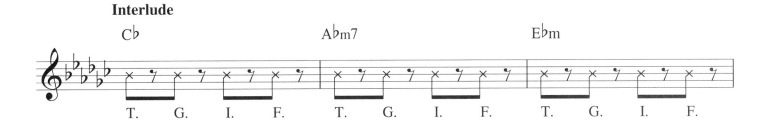

T. G. I. F. T. G. I. F. T. G. I. F.

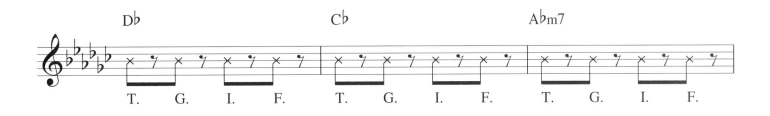

T. G. I. F. T. G. I. F. T. G. I. F.

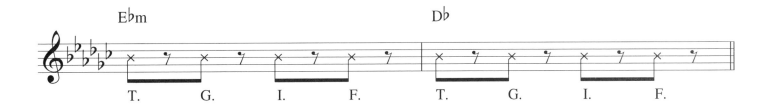

T. G. I. F. T. G. I. F.

Instrumental Solo

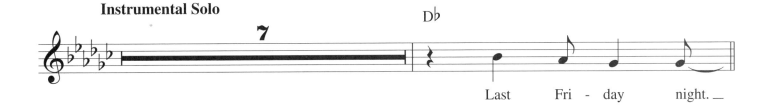

Last Fri - day night. __

Chorus

__ Yeah, we danced on tab - le - tops, and we took too man - y

shots. Think we kissed, but I for - got. Last Fri - day night. __

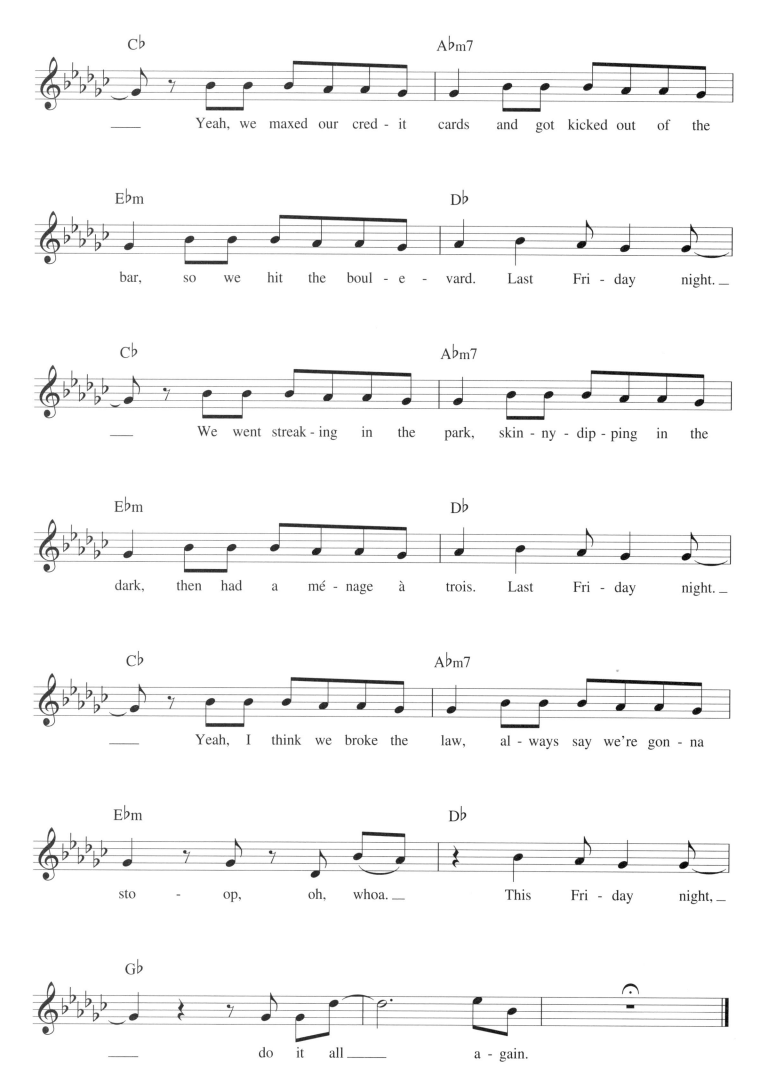

Part of Me

**Words and Music by Katy Perry, Lukasz Gottwald,
Max Martin and Bonnie McKee**

Verse

22

In fact, you can keep ev - 'ry - thing, _ yeah, _ yeah, _

Chorus

ex - cept for me. _____ This is the part of me ___ that you're nev -

- er gon - na ev - er take a - way from ___ me. ___

This is the part of me _____ that you're nev -

- er gon - na ev - er take a - way from ___ me. ___

Throw your sticks and stones, ___ throw your bombs and your blows, _

___ but you're not gon - na break ___ my soul. ___

This is the part of me _____ that you're nev -

Roar

Words and Music by Katy Perry, Lukasz Gottwald, Max Martin, Bonnie McKee and Henry Walter

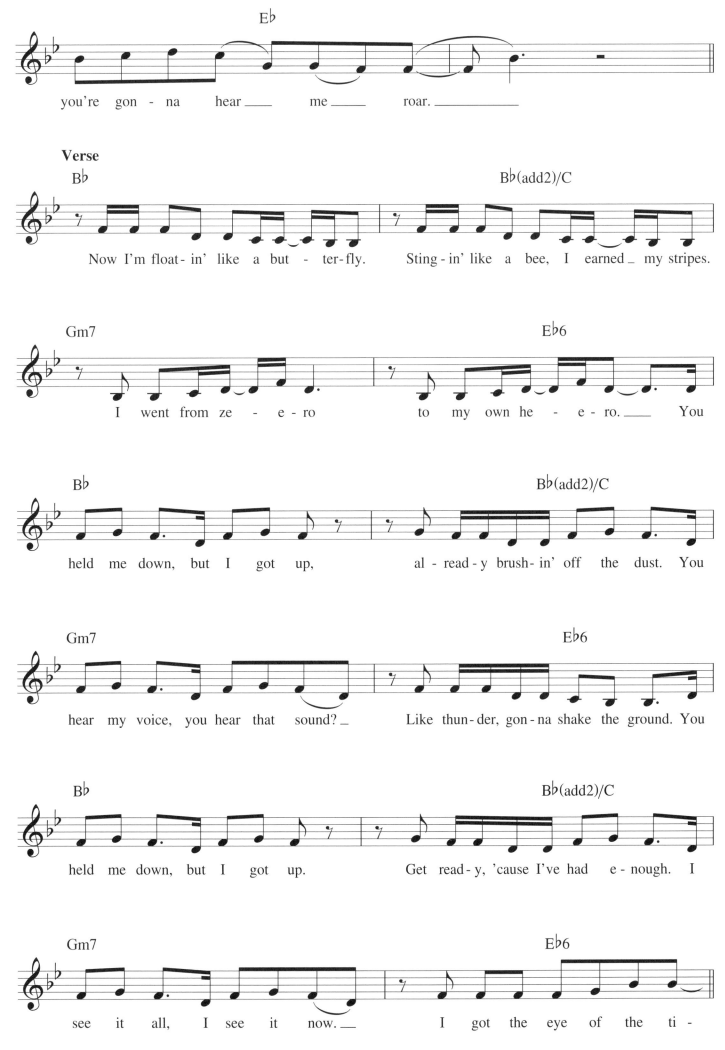

Chorus

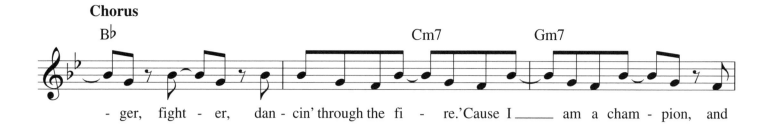

\- ger, fight - er, dan - cin' through the fi - re.'Cause I _____ am a cham - pion, and

you're gon - na hear _ me _ roar _____ loud - er, loud - er than a li - on.'Cause I _____

_____ am a cham - pion, and you're gon-na hear _ me _ roar. _____ Oh, oh, oh, oh, _____

oh, _____ oh, oh, oh, oh. _____ Oh, _____ oh, oh, oh, oh, _____

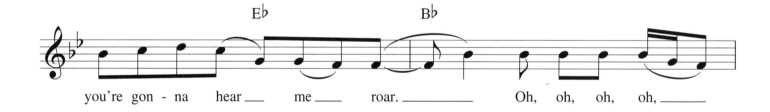

you're gon - na hear _____ me _____ roar. _____ Oh, oh, oh, oh, _____

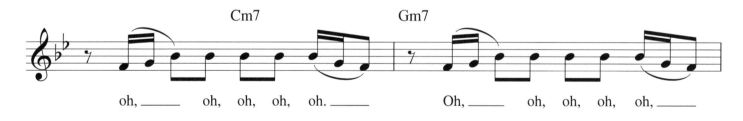

oh, _____ oh, oh, oh, oh. _____ Oh, _____ oh, oh, oh, oh, _____

Interlude

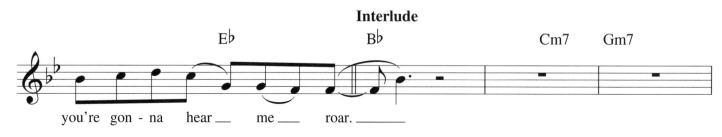

you're gon - na hear _____ me _____ roar.

F

Roar, roar, _ roar, _____ roar, _____ roar. _____

Chorus

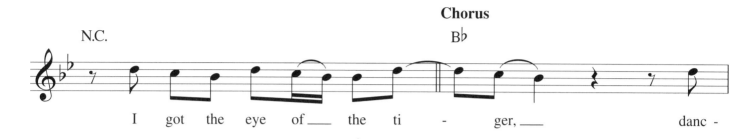

N.C.   B♭

I got the eye of __ the ti - ger, ___ danc -

Cm7   Gm7   E♭

in' through the fi - re. _____

B♭   Cm7   Gm7

Oh, ___ loud - er.

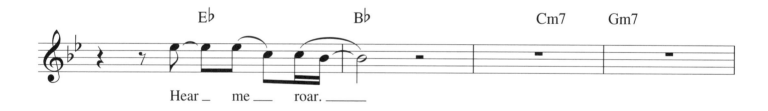

E♭   B♭   Cm7   Gm7

Hear _ me _ roar. _____

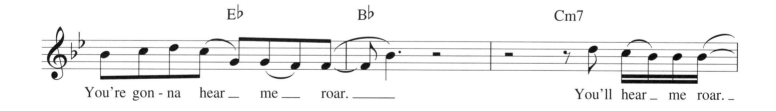

E♭   B♭   Cm7

You're gon - na hear _ me _ roar. _____   You'll hear _ me roar. _

Gm7   E♭   B♭

_____   You're gon - na hear _ me _ roar. ___

Teenage Dream

Words and Music by Katy Perry, Bonnie McKee, Lukasz Gottwald, Max Martin and Benjamin Levin

So take a chance and don't ev - er look back, don't ev - er look back. I'm a get your

heart rac - ing in my skin - tight _ jeans, be your teen - age _ dream to - night.

Let you put your hands on __ me in my skin - tight _ jeans, be your

teen - age ___ dream to - night.

Chorus

You make me feel like I'm liv - in' a teen - age dream,

The way you turn me on, I can't sleep. Let's run a - way and don't

Unconditionally

**Words and Music by Katy Perry, Lukasz Gottwald,
Max Martin and Henry Walter**

Outro

Wide Awake

Words and Music by Katy Perry, Lukasz Gottwald, Max Martin,
Henry Walter and Bonnie McKee

Chorus

44

fall - in' from _____ cloud _____ nine. _____

Bridge

_____ Thun - der rum - bl - ing,

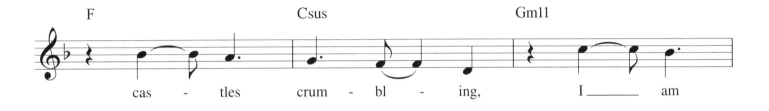

cas - tles crum - bl - ing, I _____ am

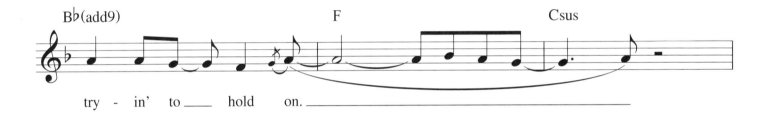

try - in' to _____ hold on. _____

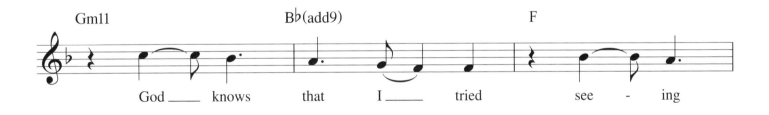

God _____ knows that I _____ tried see - ing

the bright _____ side. I'm _____ not

blind an - y - more. _____

Interlude

Oh, yeah. ____

Chorus

Fall - in' from ____ cloud ____ nine, ____

crash - ing from ____ the ____ high. ____

____ You know I'm let - ting go ____

____ to - night. _____ I'm

fall - in' from ____ cloud ____ nine. _____

Outro